WILD *about* WATERFOWL

Stoeger Publishing
Great Outdoor Books Since 1925

STOEGER PUBLISHING COMPANY
is a division of Benelli U.S.A.

Benelli U.S.A.
Vice President and General Manager: Stephen Otway
Director of Brand Marketing and Communications:
  Stephen McKelvain

Stoeger Publishing Company
President: Jeffrey Reh
Publisher: Jay Langston
Managing Editor: Harris J. Andrews
Design and Production Director: Cynthia T. Richardson
Director of Photography: Alex Bowers
Imaging Specialist: William Graves
Copy Editor: Kate Baird
Publishing Assistant: Christine Lawton
National Sales Manager: Cheryl Crowell
Sales Manager Assistant: Julie Brownlee
Assistant to the Publisher: Shannon McWilliams

Published by Stoeger Publishing Company
17603 Indian Head Highway, Suite 200
Accokeek, Maryland 20607

BK0319
ISBN:0-88317-262-3
Library of Congress Control Number: 2002110163

Manufactured in the United States of America

Distributed to the book trade and
to the sporting goods trade by:
Stoeger Industries
17603 Indian Head Highway, Suite 200
Accokeek, Maryland 20607

Fourth of six in the *Wild About* cookbooks series.

Printed in Canada

OTHER PUBLICATIONS:
SB 2004 - 95th Edition
  The World's Standard Firearms Reference Book
GTG 26th Edition
  Complete, Fully-illustrated Guide to Modern
  Firearms with Current Market Values

Hunting & Shooting
  Hounds of the World
  The Turkey Hunter's Tool Kit: Shooting Savvy
  Archer's Bible
  Hunting Whitetails East & West
  Mr. Whitetail's Trailing the Hunter's Moon
  Hunting Club Management Guide
  Complete Book of Whitetail Hunting
  Hunting and Shooting with the Modern Bow
  The Ultimate in Rifle Accuracy
  Advanced Black Powder Hunting
  Labrador Retrievers
  Hunting America's Wild Turkey
  Taxidermy Guide
  Cowboy Action Shooting
  Great Shooters of the World

Collecting Books
  Sporting Collectibles
  The Working Folding Knife
  The Lore of Spices

Firearms
  Antique Guns
  P-38 Automatic Pistol
  The Walther Handgun Story
  Complete Guide to Service Handguns
  Firearms Disassembly with Exploded Views
  Rifle Guide
  Gunsmithing at Home
  The Book of the Twenty-Two
  Complete Guide to Modern Rifles
  Complete Guide to Classic Rifles
  Legendary Sporting Rifles
  FN Browning Armorer to the World
  Modern Beretta Firearms
  How to Buy & Sell Used Guns
  Heckler & Koch: Armorers of the Free World
  Spanish Handguns

Reloading
  The Handloader's Manual of Cartridge
  Conversions
  Modern Sporting Rifle Cartridges
  Complete Reloading Guide

Fishing
  Ultimate Bass Boats
  Bassing Bible
  The Flytier's Companion
  Deceiving Trout
  The Complete Book of Trout Fishing
  The Complete Book of Flyfishing
  Peter Dean's Guide to Fly-Tying
  The Flytier's Manual
  Handbook of Fly Tying
  The Fly Fisherman's Entomological Pattern Book
  Fiberglass Rod Making
  To Rise a Trout

Motorcycles & Trucks
  The Legend of Harley-Davidson
  The Legend of the Indian
  Best of Harley-Davidson
  Classic Bikes
  Great Trucks
  4X4 Vehicles

Cooking Game
  Fish & Shellfish Care & Cookery
  Game Cookbook
  Dress 'Em Out
  Wild About Venison
  Wild About Game Birds
  Wild About Freshwater Fish

Contents

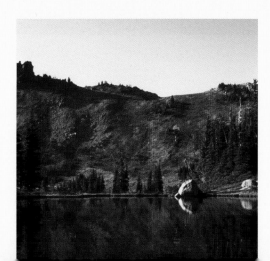

Introduction

From man's earliest origins to the present day, waterfowl and shore birds have loomed large in human diet. Primitive people ate the tasty flesh any time they could manage to catch birds. Eventually, with the development and growing sophistication of firearms, ducks and certain species of shore birds came to be considered choice gourmet fare. Widespread market hunting resulted, and highly-skilled hunters armed with shotguns and punt guns enjoyed so much success that populations declined dramatically.

What Nash Buckingham, one of the greatest waterfowlers and a revered sports writer, described as "the prodigal years" continued well into the twentieth century. Even with the passage of regulations that set seasons and ended market hunting, lax law enforcement and incredibly liberal limits (in some cases as many as 30 geese and 50 ducks per hunter per day) did little to turn the tide of declining populations. Agricultural practices that destroyed vital nesting habitats also took their toll.

Only with the passage of federal legislation to control the hunting of migratory birds, along with a sharp upsurge in conservation activism, did the first glimmer of hope appear on a bleak horizon. We will never again know the glories of yesteryear, when gabbling geese filled the sky from horizon to horizon and a noisy symphony of whistling duck wings greeted every winter dawn. Nor will we see a return to the days when tens of thousands of shorebirds teemed in coastal marshlands and hidden bays.

Yet, thanks to careful regulation, outstanding conservation work, and recognition among hunters of the importance of moderation, today's waterfowler or wingshooter can enjoy an eminently satisfying sport.

This book is a celebration of an integral and important aspect of their efforts—the culinary delights offered by ducks, geese and shore birds. Proper ethics demand that the hunter use the fruits of his sporting endeavors. For that matter, there are few things more satisfying than sitting down to a festive meal with a perfectly prepared goose, delicious ducks or a platter of shore birds gracing the table.

The pages that follow will provide you with expert guidance on how to prepare some of the finest food anyone could want.

Before we turn to the essence of this work—dozens of ways to prepare succulent waterfowl and savory shore birds—here are a few practical suggestions on the cleaning and handling of birds.

1. Unless it is exceptionally cold, field dress (remove the entrails) birds as soon as you can.
2. Plucking birds can be a tedious task, but it is recommended. Feathers are much easier to remove if plucked while the carcass is still warm. Otherwise, dip in piping hot water to loosen the feathers. Remember to singe after plucking.
3. For the best taste, eat ducks, geese, or shore birds while fresh. They can, however, be frozen if necessary.
4. If you do freeze them, be sure to clean well, wrap carefully against freezer burn and use within a few months.

In many cases it is possible to substitute one species of waterfowl for another by matching the size and dietary habits. Use the expert guidance provided in these recipes to good advantage—and *bon appetit*!

Brown Stock (Bouillon)

4 CUPS

Ingredients

2 lb	waterfowl carcasses	1 kg
3	carrots, cut into pieces	3
2	stalks celery, cut into pieces	2
2	onions, cut into pieces	2
1/4 cup	tomato paste	60 ml
2	cloves garlic	2
6-8	peppercorns	6-8
2	bay leaves	2
2	sprigs fresh thyme *or*	2
1/2 tsp	dried thyme	2 ml
1	sprig fresh parsley *or*	1
1 tsp	dried parsley	5 ml
6 cups	water	1.5 l

Method

1. In an ovenproof dish, brown the carcasses and the vegetables in the oven at 450°F (225°C) for approximately 15 minutes.
2. Add the tomato paste and bake until the entire mixture is nicely browned.
3. Transfer the mixture to a large pot. Add the remaining ingredients and bring to a boil.
4. Simmer over low heat for 1 1/2 hours.
5. Strain. Use the stock for soups and sauces.

Ducks

There are dozens of species of ducks (more than 100 worldwide), ranging from those with intriguing names like baldpates, old squaws and harlequins to those whose names obviously derive from their appearance, such as canvasbacks, golden-eyes and black ducks. As any veteran waterfowler knows, identifying ducks at a distance can be a challenging task, and when you factor in the need to distinguish between males and females of a particular species, matters become even more complex.

Some of the same complexity faces those who cook ducks. The quality of taste varies appreciably, with so-called "fish eaters" ranking much lower on the desirability scale than ducks whose diet consists primarily or exclusively of vegetation. You can tell a great deal about the likely quality of a duck by knowing which of the three broad groups—puddle ducks, diving ducks and sea ducks—it belongs to.

Puddle ducks are those able to walk on land. They are almost exclusively herbivores, and their preferred dietary items—wild rice, corn, acorns and wheat—make them a treat to eat. In terms of numbers and culinary quality, the classic puddle duck is the mallard. Equally appealing are wood ducks and those diminutive morsels of delight, the various species of teal.

On the other hand, the canvasback is a diving duck and ranks high in terms of finding favor on the table. Unlike most divers, whose diet includes a large amount of fish, mollusks and crustaceans, the canvasback feeds primarily on underwater vegetation such as wild celery. Although its numbers have declined dramatically, a pair of canvasbacks on the table, perhaps stuffed with a chestnut or cornbread and cranberry dressing, remains a gift from the gods.

Sea ducks, such as eiders and scoters, are the least desirable members of the duck clan. Since their diet consists largely of clams and mussels, they are often called "fish ducks." They can have a very strong and unappetizing flavor; however, the breast meat, when completely skinned and with all fat removed, is quite palatable. Since the preferred approach for dressing and cooking puddle ducks involves keeping the skin intact, this distinction is quite important.

When properly dressed and prepared and with due consideration for the differences between various species, any duck can provide an epicurean adventure. In the pages that follow, you have ample opportunity for many such adventures.

Strawberry-Flavoured Duck Brochettes

Ingredients

Marinade

1 carton	strawberries, washed and hulled	1 carton
1/2 cup	oil	125 ml
	juice and zest of 1 lemon	
2 tbsp	chopped fresh mint	30 ml
1 tsp	chili powder	5 ml
	freshly ground pepper to taste	

Duck

1 1/3 lb	mallard breasts, cubed	600 g
4	green onions, cut in 1-in. (2.5-cm) lengths	4
1	yellow pepper, cut into large cubes	1
	salt to taste	

Method

1. In a food processor, purée half the strawberries. Add the other marinade ingredients and mix well.
2. Transfer to a shallow dish and add the duck pieces, coating well with the strawberry mixture. Cover and marinate in the refrigerator for at least 30 minutes.
3. Preheat the barbecue to medium-high.
4. Remove the duck from the marinade and place on skewers, alternating the meat with the remaining whole strawberries, green onions and yellow pepper cubes.
5. Place the skewers on the hot grill, turning frequently so that they cook evenly. Season with salt once the meat has been seared.
6. Serve with rice and grilled seasonal vegetables.

Duck Marinated in Red Wine

Ingredients

Marinade

3/4 cup	oil	180 ml
1/2 cup	red wine	125 ml
2	shallots, chopped	2
1 or 2	cloves garlic, minced	1 or 2
2 tbsp	chopped capers	30 ml
2 tbsp	crushed coriander seeds	30 ml
	freshly ground pepper to taste	

Duck

4	wood duck legs	4
	or	
1	wood duck, cut in four (2 legs, 2 breasts)	1
	salt to taste	

Method

1. Combine all marinade ingredients in a shallow dish.

2. Add the duck pieces and coat well. Cover and marinate in the refrigerator for at least 30 minutes.

3. Preheat the barbecue to medium-high.

4. Remove the duck from the marinade, draining off any surplus.

5. Cook on an oiled barbecue grill for 20 to 30 minutes, turning only once. Season with salt once the meat has been seared.

6. Slice thinly and serve hot or cold, accompanied with a fresh vegetable salad.

Duck with Onions

Ingredients

2 tbsp	oil	**30 ml**
2 tbsp	butter	**30 ml**
1 1/3 lb	mallard breasts	**600 g**
2	onions, finely chopped	**2**
1/3 cup	white wine vinegar	**80 ml**
1/2 tsp	sugar	**2 ml**
	salt and freshly ground pepper to taste	

Method

1. Heat the oil and butter in a large skillet over high heat. Sear the duck breasts, turning only once. Season generously with salt and pepper.

2. Preheat the oven to 375 °F (190 °C).

3. Add the onions to the skillet and brown them. Meanwhile, finish cooking the duck in the oven, allowing about 8 to 15 minutes, depending on desired degree of doneness and size of breasts.

4. Remove the duck from the oven and keep warm.

5. Deglaze the skillet with the vinegar and add the sugar. Reduce until only a bit of the sauce remains. Pour over the duck breasts. Serve with your favorite starchy food and seasonal vegetables.

Note:

You can change the flavor by replacing the white wine vinegar with another vinegar, such as balsamic, for example.

Sweet and Sour Duck Soup

4 SERVINGS

Ingredients

1 tbsp	oil	**15 ml**
1/2 lb	mallard, cut into pieces	**225 g**
1	clove garlic, minced	**1**
1 tbsp	minced fresh ginger	**15 ml**
1	leek, sliced	**1**
1	carrot, sliced	**1**
1 lb	asparagus pieces	**500 g**
1	yellow pepper, cut into strips	**1**
4 cups	duck stock (see recipe on page 7)	**1 L**
1/3 lb	rice noodles	**150 g**
2 tbsp	soy sauce	**30 ml**
2 to 3 tbsp	lime juice	**30 to 45 ml**
2 tsp	hot pepper sauce, or to taste	**10 ml**
2 tbsp	cornstarch	**30 ml**

Method

1. Heat the oil in a saucepan and brown the duck pieces with the garlic and ginger. Add the leek, carrot, asparagus and pepper, and cook for 4 to 5 minutes over low heat. Add the duck stock and bring to a boil.

2. Add the noodles and cook for another 4 to 5 minutes, until the noodles are tender. Meanwhile, combine the soy sauce, lime juice and hot pepper sauce. Add this mixture to the hot soup.

3. Thicken with the cornstarch mixed with a bit of water and season to taste.

4. Ladle the soup into bowls and serve hot.

Duck Breast
with Beet Chutney

Ingredients

Chutney

1	apple or pear, peeled and thinly sliced	1
1	onion, thinly sliced	1
1	clove garlic, crushed	1
1/4 tsp	crushed chilies	1 ml
1/2 stick	cinnamon	1/2 stick
1/2 tsp	salt	2 ml
1	clove	1
1/2 tsp	freshly ground black pepper	2 ml
1/2 tsp	chopped fresh ginger	2 ml
1/2 cup	cider vinegar	125 ml
2	large beets, cooked and cubed	2
1/4 cup	brown sugar	60 ml
2 tbsp	golden raisins	30 ml
1/4 cup	chopped fresh parsley	60 ml

Duck

4	green-winged teal breasts	4
	or	
1	green-winged teal, cut into four (2 legs, 2 breasts)	1
	salt and freshly ground pepper, to taste	

Method

1. In a large saucepan, combine all but the last four chutney ingredients.
2. Bring to a boil and simmer over low heat for 15 to 20 minutes.
3. Add the beets, brown sugar and raisins and continue cooking for 15 minutes. Season to taste.
4. Preheat the barbecue to medium-high or the oven to 400°F (200°C).
5. Cook the teal breasts or pieces for 25 to 30 minutes.
6. Add the parsley to the chutney and serve with the teal.

Raspberry Duck

Ingredients

1 tsp	oil	5 ml
2	black duck breasts, skin on	2
	salt and freshly ground pepper to taste	
1	shallot, minced	1
1/4 cup	raspberry vinegar	60 ml
1/4 cup	white wine	60 ml
1 cup	duck or waterfowl stock (see recipe on page 7)	250 ml
1	sprig fresh rosemary	1
	or	
1/2 tsp	dried rosemary	2 ml
3/4 cup	puréed and strained raspberries	180 ml
1 tsp	cornstarch	5 ml

Method

1. Preheat the oven to 190°F (375°C).
2. Heat the oil in a skillet and sear the duck breasts on both sides, skin side first. Season with salt and pepper, place in a baking dish, and continue cooking in the oven for 15 to 20 minutes.
3. Remove the duck from the oven and keep warm.
4. Brown the shallot in the same skillet and deglaze with the vinegar and wine. Reduce the liquid by half.
5. Add the stock and the rosemary. Season to taste and simmer for 3 or 4 minutes.
6. Add the raspberries and reduce the stock by a third.
7. Thicken with cornstarch mixed with a bit of water and season to taste.
8. Slice the breasts and serve with the sauce.

Breast of Duck in a Cheese Sauce

Ingredients

1 1/3 lb	boned pintail duck breasts	600 g
	salt and freshly ground pepper to taste	

Cheese Sauce

2	shallots, chopped	2
1/2 cup	white wine	125 ml
1 cup	brown duck stock or beef stock	250 ml
1	sprig fresh rosemary	1
1	sprig fresh thyme	1
2 tsp	softened butter	10 ml
2 tsp	flour	10 ml
1/3 lb	cheese of your choice, coarsely chopped (Swiss, Gouda, Havarti)	150 g

Method

1. Preheat the oven to 350°F (180°C).

2. Place the duck breasts in a hot skillet and sear quickly, skin side down first, 1 to 2 minutes per side.

3. Transfer the duck to an ovenproof dish, skin side up, season with salt and pepper, and continue cooking in the oven, uncovered, for 10 to 12 minutes.

4. Meanwhile, brown the shallots in the same skillet for 2 minutes or until golden.

5. Deglaze with the wine and reduce by a third, about 2 to 3 minutes.

6. Pour in the stock and add the sprigs of rosemary and thyme. Simmer for 4 or 5 minutes, reducing again by a third.

7. Combine the butter with the flour to make a *beurre manié*. Whisk the butter mixture into the sauce and simmer for 4 to 5 minutes. Whisk until the sauce thickens and the floury taste has disappeared. Remove the rosemary and thyme and season to taste.

8. Gradually melt the cheese into the sauce, whisking until smooth.

9. Serve the duck breasts sliced decoratively and garnish with a thin stream of sauce. Accompany this tasty dish with a starchy food and seasonal vegetables.

Duck with Cherry Balsamic Vinegar Glaze

4 SERVINGS

Ingredients

Marinade

1/2 cup	oil	125 ml
1/4 cup	balsamic vinegar	60 ml
2 tbsp	chopped fresh basil	30 ml
	freshly ground pepper to taste	
1	mallard duck, quartered (2 legs, 2 breasts)	1

Glaze

1 tbsp	butter	15 ml
1	shallot, minced	1
1	clove garlic, minced	1
1 cup	fresh or canned pitted cherries	250 ml
1/4 cup	balsamic vinegar	60 ml
2 tbsp	maple syrup or honey	30 ml
1 to 2 tbsp	chopped fresh basil	15 to 30 ml
	salt and freshly ground pepper to taste	

Method

1. Combine all marinade ingredients in a shallow dish. Add the duck pieces, cover and marinate in the refrigerator for at least 30 minutes, or up to 6 hours.

2. Preheat the oven to 425°F (210°C). Remove the duck from the marinade, place on a baking sheet and bake in the center of the oven for 25 to 30 minutes.

3. Meanwhile, heat the butter in a skillet and brown the shallot and garlic for 2 minutes, or until tender.

4. Deglaze with the balsamic vinegar and reduce until almost dry.

5. Add the maple syrup or honey and the basil, once cooking is completed. Season to taste.

6. Serve the duck either hot or cold, topped with the glaze.

Note:

The glaze can be prepared in advance, and you can substitute black currants, gooseberries, cranberries, etc., for the cherries.

Duck Sautée à l'italienne

Ingredients

1 tbsp	oil	15 ml
1 tbsp	butter	15 ml
1 1/3 lb	mallard breasts, sliced	600 g
1	onion, chopped	1
2	cloves garlic, chopped	2
1/4 cup	white wine or water	60 ml
1 can (19 oz)	crushed tomatoes	1 can (540 ml)
1	bay leaf	1
	salt and freshly ground pepper to taste	
	Parmesan cheese shavings to taste	

Method

1. Heat the oil and butter in a skillet over medium-high heat.
2. Sauté the duck slices for 2 to 3 minutes to sear. Remove and keep warm.
3. In the same skillet, cook the onion and garlic.
4. Deglaze with the white wine and reduce the liquid until almost dry.
5. Add the tomatoes and the bay leaf and season to taste. Bring to a boil and simmer for 5 to 10 minutes.
6. Arrange the duck slices over the sauce and garnish with Parmesan cheese shavings.

Duck Canapés
with Blueberry Onion Confit

Ingredients

Blueberry onion confit

1 tbsp	butter	15 ml
1	red onion, thinly sliced	1
1 cup	fresh or frozen blueberries	250 ml
1/2 cup	white wine	125 ml
1/2 cup	sugar	125 ml
1	bay leaf	1
	pinch dried thyme	
	pinch dried rosemary	
	salt and freshly ground pepper to taste	
1/2 lb	shredded redhead duck confit	225 g
	or homemade rillettes	
	or homemade liver mousse	
	a selection of crackers or toasted bread slices	
	fresh herbs and blueberries for garnish	

Method

1. Heat the butter in a saucepan and brown the onions over medium heat until tender. Add the blueberries and cook for another 2 minutes.

2. Deglaze with the white wine and reduce by half.

3. Stir in the sugar, bay leaf, thyme and rosemary. Allow the onions to caramelize and reduce the liquid until almost dry.

4. Season to taste and let cool.

5. Garnish crackers or toast slices with the duck confit.

6. Place a spoonful of the blueberry onion confit on top of the duck and garnish with fresh blueberries and herbs.

Note:

To keep the blueberry onion confit fresh longer, transfer it to sterilized jars and keep in the refrigerator, or preserve using the traditional canning method.

Grilled Duck
with Roasted Garlic

Ingredients

1	bulb garlic	1
1 to 2 tbsp	oil	15 to 30 ml
1 cup	duck stock	250 ml
3 tbsp	soy sauce	45 ml
1/4 cup	tomato paste	60 ml
	coarsely ground pepper	
1 1/3 lb	wood duck breasts	600 g

Method

1. Preheat the barbecue to medium-high or the oven to 350°F (180°C).

2. Cut off the top of the garlic bulb to reveal all the cloves. Place the bulb on a square of aluminum foil, drizzle with oil, seal the foil and roast for 20 to 25 minutes or until the cloves are tender.

3. Peel the garlic cloves and purée.

4. Meanwhile, in a small saucepan, reduce the stock with the soy sauce and tomato paste over medium heat until the sauce thickens. Add the crushed peppercorns and the puréed garlic.

5. Baste the duck with the roast garlic sauce and grill on a hot barbecue. This dish is best when the meat is still slightly pink.

Duck Breast
with Rosemary Sauce

Ingredients

4	mallard breasts, boned	**4**

Sauce		
2	shallots, chopped	**2**
1/2 cup	red wine	**125 ml**
1 cup	duck stock (see recipe on page 7)	**250 ml**
1	sprig fresh rosemary	**1**
1 tbsp	softened butter	**15 ml**
1 tbsp	flour	**15 ml**
	salt and freshly ground pepper to taste	

Method

1. Preheat the barbecue to medium-high.

2. Cook the duck breasts for about twenty minutes, turning only once.

3. Meanwhile, cook the shallots in a skillet, over medium heat (1 to 2 minutes).

4. Deglaze with the wine, and reduce by a third.

5. Moisten with the stock and add the rosemary. Reduce by a third again.

6. Combine the butter and flour to obtain a *beurre manié*.

7. Stir the *beurre manié* into the sauce with a whisk, bring to a boil and simmer for several minutes until the sauce thickens and the floury taste has been cooked off.

8. Remove the rosemary sprig and season to taste.

9. Serve the duck garnished with a ribbon of the sauce. Accompany this tasty dish with a starch-based food and seasonal vegetables.

Duck with Pink Peppercorns

Ingredients

1	black duck, whole	1
1	onion, chopped	1
	Sauce	
1 tbsp	butter	15 ml
1	shallot, minced	1
1/2 cup	white wine	125 ml
1 cup	duck stock (see recipe on page 7)	250 ml
2 tbsp	whole pink peppercorns	30 ml
1 tbsp	flour	15 ml
1 tbsp	softened butter	15 ml
	salt, to taste	

Method

1. Preheat the oven to 350°F (180°C).

2. Spread the chopped onion in a roasting pan and place the duck on top. Cook in the centre of the oven for 60 to 75 minutes, basting often with the cooking juices.

3. Meanwhile, prepare the sauce. Heat the butter in a small saucepan and cook the shallot. Deglaze with the wine and reduce by a third.

4. Add the stock and the peppercorns, and reduce by a third.

5. Combine the butter with the flour to make a *beurre manié*.

6. Whisk in the *beurre manié* and continue cooking for 3 to 5 minutes.

7. Season to taste. Serve the duck coated with the sauce.

Bavarian Duck

Method

1. Mix all marinade ingredients together in a shallow dish. Add the duck pieces, cover, and marinate in the refrigerator for at least 30 minutes, or for up to 6 hours.

2. Remove the meat from the marinade and dredge in the flour.

3. Heat the oil and butter in a saucepan and sear the duck pieces on all sides.

4. Add the marinade, bring to a boil and simmer for 20 to 30 minutes. Season to taste.

5. Serve with a starchy food and, seasonal vegetables.

Ingredients

Marinade

1 cup	duck stock (see recipe on page 7)	250 ml
12-oz. bottle	beer	341 ml bottle
1/3 cup	honey	80 ml
2 tbsp	chopped fresh ginger	30 ml
	pinch ground cinnamon	
	pinch cayenne	
	freshly ground pepper to taste	

Duck

1	redhead duck, cut into pieces	1
1/4 cup	flour	60 ml
2 tbsp	oil	30 ml
1 tbsp	butter	15 ml
	salt to taste	

Warm Duck Liver Salad
with Port

4 SERVINGS

Ingredients

1 tbsp	oil	15 ml
1 tbsp	butter	15 ml
1	carrot, thinly sliced or julienned	1
12	asparagus tips, blanched	12
1/2	red onion, sliced	1/2
1	clove garlic, minced	1
1/2 lb	black duck liver, cleaned and sliced	225 g
1/3 cup	port wine	80 ml
	juice of 1/2 lemon	
2 cups	washed and shredded lettuce of your choice	500 ml
	salt and freshly ground pepper to taste	

Method

1. Heat the oil and butter in a skillet, add the carrots and asparagus and cook over medium heat until the carrots are tender. Remove the vegetables and set aside.

2. In the same skillet, sauté the onion and garlic over high heat.

3. Add the sliced duck liver and cook for 3 to 4 minutes (do not overcook the liver).

4. Deglaze with the port and reduce over low heat for 1 minute.

5. Add the lemon juice and season to taste.

6. Divide the shredded lettuce among 4 serving plates, making a nest in the center, and place the vegetables on top.

7. Garnish each plate with the deglazed liver and use the port-lemon mixture as a vinaigrette for the duck liver salad. Serve immediately.

Liver Mousse

Ingredients

1	shallot	1
1	clove garlic, chopped	1
1 tbsp	oil	15 ml
1 tbsp	butter	15 ml
1/2 lb	wigeon or other waterfowl liver	225 g
1	apple, peeled and cubed	1
1 tbsp	cider vinegar	15 ml
1/4 cup	white wine	60 ml
1/3 cup	softened butter	80 ml
1/2 cup	whipping cream	125 ml
	your choice of fresh herbs (rosemary, tarragon, basil)	
	salt and freshly ground pepper to taste	

Method

1. Heat the oil and butter in a skillet. Add the shallot and garlic, and sauté over medium-high heat.
2. Add the liver pieces and brown over high heat.
3. Add the apple and continue cooking for 2 minutes.
4. Deglaze with the vinegar and wine, and reduce by half. Remove from the heat and allow to cool.
5. Once cooled, purée in a food processor until smooth.
6. Add the butter and transfer the mixture to a bowl. Stir in the cream with a spatula.
7. Season to taste and add your favorite herbs. Refrigerate for at least 1 hour.
8. Serve as is, or in decorative molds, with toast and crackers.

Note:

To mold the liver mousse, transfer to ramekins or a decorative mold. Refrigerate for several hours and, when ready to serve, dip the mold in hot water so that the mousse slides out more easily.

Duck with Sweet Potato Purée

4 SERVINGS

Ingredients

3 cups	peeled and cubed sweet potatoes or yams	**750 ml**
1 cup	peeled and cubed potatoes	**250 ml**
1	onion, finely chopped	**1**
2	cloves garlic, sliced	**2**
2 tbsp	finely chopped fresh ginger	**30 ml**
2 tbsp	chopped fresh tarragon	**30 ml**
2 tbsp	butter	**30 ml**
1	wigeon, whole	**1**
3/4 cup	apple jelly	**180 ml**
1/4 tsp	crushed chilies	**1 ml**
	salt and freshly ground pepper to taste	

Method

1. Place the yams, potatoes, onion, garlic and ginger in a large saucepan. Cover with water, bring to a boil and simmer until the vegetables are tender.

2. Preheat the oven to 375°F (190°C).

3. Drain the cooked vegetables and set aside 1 cup (250 ml) of the cooking liquid. Mash the vegetables using a potato masher. Add the tarragon and butter. If the purée is too thick, add some of the reserved cooking liquid. Season to taste.

4. Place the wigeon in an ovenproof dish, breast side up. Fill the bird's cavity with the potato purée.

5. Melt the apple jelly in a small saucepan with the crushed chilies, and baste the duck with this mixture.

6. Cook in the oven for 60 to 75 minutes, basting the duck every 15 minutes. Serve the duck accompanied with the purée.

Duck à la Provençale

Ingredients

Marinade

1	redhead, whole	1
1/2 cup	white wine	125 ml
2 tbsp	lemon juice	30 ml
1	onion, chopped	1
1 or 2	cloves garlic, minced	1 or 2
2 tbsp	your choice of fresh chopped herbs (thyme, oregano, basil, parsley, etc.)	30 ml
1/3 cup	sliced black or green olives	80 ml
1/3 cup	sun-dried tomatoes preserved in oil or rehydrated, chopped	80 ml
	salt and freshly ground pepper to taste	

Method

1. Preheat the oven to 350°F (180°C).
2. Place the duck in a large saucepan. Add the white wine and cover with water. Season generously.
3. Bring to a boil and simmer for 30 minutes. Remove the duck from the saucepan and place on a baking sheet.
4. Mix all remaining ingredients and coat the duck with this mixture.
5. Roast in the center of the oven for 30 minutes.
6. Transfer the duck to a serving platter and carve at the table.

Sesame-Roasted Duck

Ingredients

Marinade

1/4 cup	grilled sesame oil	60 ml
1 or 2	cloves garlic, chopped	1 or 2
1 tbsp	chopped fresh ginger	15 ml
2 tbsp	rice or cider vinegar	30 ml
2 tbsp	soy sauce	30 ml
1 cup	garlic sauce for spare ribs	250 ml
3	green onions, chopped	3

Duck

1	pintail duck, cut into pieces	1
2 tbsp	sesame seeds, regular or toasted	30 ml

Method

1. Combine all ingredients in a shallow dish. Place the duck on top, cover and marinate in the refrigerator for at least 1 hour, or for up to 6 hours.

2. Preheat the oven to 425°F (210°C).

3. Drain the duck well and transfer the marinade to a skillet. Place the duck in an ovenproof dish and roast for 15 to 20 minutes. Meanwhile, bring the marinade to a boil for 5 minutes and add the sesame seeds. Reduce by half.

4. Add the duck pieces to the sauce and continue cooking until well glazed.

5. Serve with sautéed vegetables and rice noodles.

Duck and Shrimp Vermicelli

Ingredients

4 oz	rice vermicelli	120 g
3 tbsp	oil	45 ml
1/2 lb	boned black duck pieces	225 g
1	onion, sliced	1
1	red pepper, cut into strips	1
1 cup	snow peas	250 ml
6	green onions, cut into segments	6
1 tbsp	chopped fresh ginger	15 ml
24	raw shrimp, peeled	24
1/2 cup	duck stock	125 ml
1 tsp	curry paste	5 ml
3 tbsp	soy sauce	45 ml
1 tbsp	toasted sesame oil	15 ml
1	beaten egg, cooked as an omelette and shredded	1

Method

1. Cook the rice vermicelli in boiling water for 1 minute. Drain, rinse under cold water, drain again and cut into 4-in. (10-cm) sections. Set aside.

2. In a skillet or a wok, heat the oil over high heat and sauté the duck pieces. Remove and set aside.

3. In the same skillet, brown the vegetables. Remove and set aside with the duck.

4. Sauté the shrimp in the same skillet, remove and set aside with the vegetables and duck.

5. Deglaze the skillet with the stock. Add the curry, soy sauce and sesame oil, and mix well.

6. Add the vermicelli and cook over high heat until the vermicelli is evenly coated with sauce, about 1 minute.

7. Then add the duck, vegetables, shrimp and shredded omelette. Transfer to dinner plates and serve immediately.

Grilled Marinated Duck

Ingredients

Marinade

1/2	onion, chopped	1/2
1	clove garlic, chopped	1
2 tbsp	olive oil	30 ml
1/4 cup	Pineau des Charentes or other aperitif wine	60 ml
	juice of 1 lemon	
1 tsp	fresh rosemary *or*	5 ml
2 tsp	dried rosemary	10 ml
	freshly ground pepper to taste	
1	black duck, cut into eight pieces	1

Method

1. Mix all the marinade ingredients in a large shallow dish.

2. Add the duck pieces and stir well to coat. Cover and marinate in the refrigerator for 2 hours, turning the pieces twice.

3. Preheat the barbecue to medium-high or the oven to 350°F (180°C).

4. Remove the duck pieces from the marinade, drain well and cook on the grill or in the oven for 10 to 15 minutes per side. Serve immediately.

Smoked Duck Breast

Ingredients

Seasoning

2 tbsp	fresh herbs (rosemary, basil, thyme)	**30 ml**
	or	
2 tsp	dried herbs	**10 ml**
	freshly ground pepper to taste	
4	pintail duck breasts	**4**
3 cups	untreated wood chips (maple, cherry, hickory)	**750 ml**

Method

1. Mix all seasoning ingredients together in a shallow dish.

2. Place the duck pieces in the dish and coat well with the seasoning. Cover and refrigerate for about 24 hours.

3. Soak the wood chips in cold water for 30 to 60 minutes before cooking.

4. Drain the wood chips and wrap in aluminum foil. Pierce the foil in several places with a fork.

5. Place the chips under a gas barbecue grill and heat to medium-high for 7 or 8 minutes, or until you see smoke escaping from the foil. Shut off one burner and adjust the other side to low.

6. Remove the duck pieces from the seasoning mixture and place on the side of the barbecue that has been turned off. Leave to smoke for 1 hour to 1 1/4 hours. Do not let the duck brown.

7. Set aside to cool and serve in very thin slices.

Note:

Duck can also be smoked using a charcoal or electric smoker.

Crispy Szechuan-Style Duck

Ingredients

1/4 cup	corn flour	60 ml
3 tbsp	cornmeal	45 ml
1/2+1/4 tsp	Chinese 5-spice powder	2+1 ml
1 lb	skinned teal pieces	500 g
1/2 cup	chicken or duck stock	125 ml
2 tsp	sugar	10 ml
1 tbsp	soy sauce	15 ml
1/2 tsp	sesame oil	2 ml
1 tbsp	rice vinegar	15 ml
1 cup	canola or peanut oil for frying	250 ml
	hot peppers, dried, seeds removed, to taste	
2	cloves garlic, chopped	2
2 tsp	chopped fresh ginger	10 ml
4	green onions, cut into 2-in. (5-cm) lengths	4
1 tbsp	cornstarch	15 ml
	salt and freshly ground pepper to taste	

Method

1. Mix the corn flour, cornmeal and 1/2 tsp (2 ml) of the spices in a small bowl, and season to taste. Coat the duck pieces with this mixture, dusting off any surplus. Set aside.

2. Mix together the stock, sugar, soy sauce, sesame oil, vinegar, and the remainder of the spices, and season to taste. Set aside.

3. Heat the oil in a wok over very high heat and brown the duck pieces in three batches. Drain and place on an absorbent towel.

4. Remove the surplus oil from the wok, leaving about 1 tbsp (15 ml). Add the hot peppers, garlic and ginger, browning evenly.

5. Add the green onion and continue sautéing for several seconds.

6. Add the stock and bring to a boil.

7. Thicken with the cornstarch mixed with a bit of water, and season to taste.

Serve the duck pieces accompanied with the sauce.

Layered Duck and Pepper Squash with Bulgur

4 SERVINGS

Ingredients

2 tbsp	oil	**30 ml**
1 lb	wood duck	**500 g**
2	small leeks, sliced	**2**
2	cloves garlic, crushed	**2**
1 3/4 cups	crushed tomatoes	**430 ml**
1/4 tsp	dried basil	**1 ml**
1/4 tsp	dried thyme	**1 ml**
1 cup	bulgur	**250 ml**
2	pepper squash, peeled and sliced	**2**
1 cup	grated Swiss cheese	**250 ml**
	salt and freshly ground pepper to taste	

Method

1. Preheat the oven to 350°F (180°C).
2. Heat the oil in a skillet and brown the meat for 4 to 5 minutes. Remove and set aside.
3. Using the same skillet, cook the leeks and garlic in the remaining grease. Remove and set aside.
4. Add the tomatoes and herbs and bring to a boil.
5. Add the bulgur, cover and let simmer for 15 minutes. Season to taste; add the leek and garlic mixture and the duck.
6. Layer the squash slices in a greased ovenproof dish, followed with a layer of the duck bulgur mixture. Repeat this process, ending with a layer of pepper squash. Cover with the grated cheese and cook in the center of the oven for 30 to 35 minutes.

Note:

This recipe can also be made with other waterfowl. You can also prepare it with any leftover cooked waterfowl (omitting Step 2).

Duck à l'orange

Ingredients

1	mallard, whole	**1**
2	carrots, cut into sections	**2**
2	stalks celery, cut into sections	**2**
1	large onion, chopped	**1**
1 or 2	cloves	**1 or 2**
5 to 10	peppercorns	**5 to 10**
pinch	dried thyme	**pinch**
1 or 2	bay leaves	**1 or 2**
3 tbsp	orange juice concentrate	**45 ml**
3 tbsp	honey	**45 ml**
3 tbsp	tamari or soy sauce	**45 ml**

Sauce

2 tbsp	sugar	**30 ml**
2 tbsp	cider vinegar	**30 ml**
	juice and zest of 2 oranges	
1 1/2 cups	duck stock (see recipe on page 7)	**375 ml**
1 tbsp	tomato paste	**15 ml**
	orange sections	
	salt and freshly ground pepper to taste	

Method

1. Cover the duck with cold water in a large saucepan, add the vegetables and seasoning, cover and bring to a boil over high heat.

2. Reduce the heat to medium and simmer for 30 to 45 minutes, depending on the size of the duck.

3. Preheat the oven to 400°F (200°C).

4. In a small saucepan, mix together the orange juice concentrate, honey and tamari sauce. Cook over low heat until the honey has dissolved, and set aside.

5. Remove the duck from the stock and place in a roasting pan.

6. Brush the duck with the honey mixture, and roast in the oven for 20 to 25 minutes, basting the duck several times.

7. Meanwhile, prepare the sauce. In a small saucepan, combine the sugar and vinegar together. Cook over low heat until the sugar has dissolved and the mixture turns an amber color.

8. Add the remaining ingredients and cook until desired texture is reached. Season to taste.

9. Serve the duck accompanied with the sauce, and garnish with the orange sections.

Note:

You can freeze the remaining stock the duck was cooked in (white stock), and use it to prepare delicious soups and sauces.

Duck with a Shallot Reduction

Ingredients

1 tbsp	oil	**15 ml**
1 tbsp	butter	**15 ml**
1/2 cup	shallots, chopped	**125 ml**
1/4 cup	white wine	**60 ml**
1 cup	duck stock (see recipe on page 7)	**250 ml**
4	teal breasts	**4**
	or	
1	teal, quartered (2 legs, 2 breasts)	**1**
	salt and freshly ground pepper to taste	

Method

1. Heat the oil and butter in a skillet over medium heat.
2. Add the shallots and cook until translucent.
3. Stir in the wine and reduce until all the liquid has evaporated.
4. Add the stock and reduce by half. Season to taste.
5. Meanwhile, in another skillet, sear the teal pieces, skin side first, for 5 minutes each side, turning only once. Season to taste.
6. Transfer to a serving dish and serve with the shallot reduction.

Geese

Four species of geese are hunted in North America, with the Canada goose being by far the most important. There are no less than seven subspecies of Canada goose. They are all quite similar in appearance but can vary greatly in weight. The other species are the white-fronted goose (more commonly called the specklebelly), the prolific snow goose and the brant. The latter, while a goose, looks more like a duck, with its short neck and relatively small size.

As holds true for ducks, the edibility of geese is directly related to what they have been eating. Canadas or specklebellies that have enjoyed a steady diet of corn or rice for weeks can be delicious. One of the most common mistakes is to assume that because it is a big bird, it will require a very long cooking time.

In reality, the wild goose is a lean bird with dark meat (since it spends a great deal of time in the air), and the assumption that it requires a cooking time comparable to that for a domestic goose is erroneous. Wild goose is best served when the meat is still pink and juicy. If cooked until well done, it will be overcooked, which is the reason for most comments to the effect that goose is invariably "tough and dry." Rare to medium-rare is the way to go with breast meat and, cooked this way, a young Canada or a specklebelly is remarkably similar to a fine cut of beef.

The legs and thighs of mature geese can be tough. The solution is a simple and delicious one: use these parts, along with the wings and neck, if desired, to make salads, patés, soups or casseroles. Also, don't overlook the fact that the liver and heart can be used to make paté or wildfowl spreads.

With resident flocks of Canada geese now common over much of North America (in some areas they have become a real nuisance), hunters no longer have to live along one of the major flyways to enjoy this wonderful wingshooting sport. And, by logical extension, they now also have the opportunity to enjoy a healthy, hearty red meat. These recipes reveal the secrets of such enjoyment.

Goose Rillettes

Ingredients

1	5-lb (2-kg) snow goose, skinned and boned	1
2	bay leaves	2
1	sprig fresh thyme	1
	or	
1 tsp	dried thyme	5 ml
	duck fat, to cover	
	salt and freshly ground pepper to taste	

Method

1. Preheat the oven to 250°F (125°C).
2. Cut the goose meat into strips and season to taste.
3. Place the goose strips in an ovenproof baking dish and add the remaining ingredients. Cover and cook in the center of the oven for 4 hours.
4. Drain the goose pieces and set aside the fat.
5. Break up and shred the strips, using a fork.
6. Transfer to a mold, pack in firmly and cover with the reserved fat. Allow to cool.

Note:

Rillettes, traditionaly made with poultry or pork meat, are a sort of pâté made of chopped meat which cooks in its own fat.

When well covered with fat and stored in a sealed container, rillettes will keep in the refrigerator for several months.

Goose Liver Flan
with Red Pepper Coulis

This recipe can be made with any waterfowl liver, depending on what is available. However, it is important to respect the indicated quantities. Why not combine a variety of livers to enhance the flavor of this flan?

Ingredients

1/2 lb	Canada goose liver, trimmed	225 g
1 cup	goose stock	250 ml
1/3 cup	cottage cheese	80 ml
2	eggs	2
1/3 cup	milk	80 ml
1/4 cup	grated Parmesan	60 ml
pinch	nutmeg	pinch
	salt and freshly ground pepper to taste	

Coulis		
2	red peppers, cubed	2
2 tbsp	oil	30 ml
1/4 cup	balsamic vinegar	60 ml
	salt and freshly ground pepper to taste	

Method

1. Preheat the oven to 350°F (180°C).

2. In a saucepan, poach the livers over low heat for 10 to 15 minutes. Allow to cool in the pan and drain.

3. In a food processor, purée the livers with the cottage cheese until smooth.

4. Add the remaining ingredients, mix well and season to taste. Place the mixture in 4 buttered ramekins, and place the ramekins in an ovenproof dish half filled with water. Cook in the center of the oven for 30 to 45 minutes.

5. Meanwhile, heat the oil in a skillet and cook the peppers over low heat until tender. Deglaze with the vinegar and reduce the liquid by half or more.

6. Puree the mixture in a food processor, season to taste and keep warm.

7. Unmold the ramekins in the center of a serving dish and garnish with a spoonful of pepper coulis.

Note:

The better the quality of the balsamic vinegar for the pepper coulis, the less you will have to reduce the liquid.

Goose with Sweet Garlic Sauce

4 SERVINGS

Ingredients

1 1/3 lb	boned snow goose pieces	600 g
2 tbsp	oil	30 ml
4	cloves garlic	4
1/2 cup	milk or 10% cream	125 ml
1 tbsp	oil	15 ml
2	shallots, chopped	2
1/2 cup	red wine	125 ml
1 1/2 cups	goose stock	375 ml
1 tbsp	flour	15 ml
1 tbsp	softened butter	15 ml
	salt and freshly ground pepper to taste	

Method

1. Preheat the oven to 400°F (200°C).

2. Place the goose meat on a baking sheet, brush with oil and season to taste. Bake in the center of the oven for 35 to 40 minutes, or until the meat separates easily from the bones.

3. Meanwhile, in a small saucepan, simmer the garlic cloves in the milk until they are tender, 10 to 12 minutes. Remove the garlic from the milk and set aside.

4. Heat the oil in a skillet and sauté the shallots for 2 to 3 minutes.

5. Deglaze with the red wine and reduce by half.

6. Add the stock and reduce by a third, then add the garlic cloves.

7. Meanwhile, combine the butter with the flour to make a *beurre manié*. Thicken the sauce with the *beurre manié*, whisking vigorously.

8. Simmer 3 or 4 minutes or until the sauce is thick and smooth. Season to taste.

Serve the goose coated with the sauce.

Goose à la Créole

4 SERVINGS

Ingredients

2 tbsp	oil or butter	30 ml
2 tbsp	flour	30 ml
1 1/3 lb	Canada goose, cut into pieces	600 g
1 cup	cubed onions	250 ml
1/2	green pepper, cubed	1/2
1	celery stalk, cubed	1
2	cloves garlic, chopped	2
1 can (19 oz)	crushed tomatoes	1 can (540 ml)
1 cup	goose stock	250 ml
1	bay leaf	1
1/2 tsp	dried thyme	2 ml
	zest of 1 lemon	
1/2 tsp	freshly ground pepper	2 ml
1 tbsp	cornstarch	15 ml
	salt and freshly ground pepper to taste	

Method

1. Preheat the oven to 350°F (180°C).

2. Heat the oil in an ovenproof saucepan, add the flour and cook until the flour starts to brown.

3. Sauté the goose pieces and vegetables for 5 to 10 minutes, until golden brown.

4. Add the tomatoes and stock, and bring to a boil.

5. Stir in the remaining ingredients, except the cornstarch. Cover and cook in the center of the oven for 35 to 40 minutes, or until the meat separates easily from the bone.

6. Remove from the oven. Mix the cornstarch thoroughly with a bit of cold water and add to the sauce to thicken over medium-high heat. Season to taste.

7. Serve immediately, accompanied with small cornbread muffins.

Pan-Fried Goose Liver

This recipe is adapted from a very old Alsatian dish.

Ingredients

3 tbsp	butter	**45 ml**
4	slices whole wheat bread	**4**
1/2 lb	snow goose livers, trimmed flour	**225 g**
1/2 cup	aperitif wine (port, Pineau des Charentes, etc.)	**125 ml**
1/4 cup	brown veal or chicken stock	**60 ml**
20	green grapes	**20**
2 tbsp	cold butter cubes	**30 ml**
	salt and freshly ground pepper to taste	

Method

1. Heat the butter in a skillet over medium heat and brown the bread slices on both sides. Remove and set aside.
2. Cut the livers into 1/2-in (1-cm) slices, dredge in flour and season to taste.
3. In the same skillet, brown the liver on all sides with the butter remaining in the skillet. Remove the liver and set aside.
4. Deglaze with the port and reduce by a quarter.
5. Stir in the stock and continue cooking for 5 minutes.
6. Add the grapes and continue cooking for 2 minutes.
7. Add the cold butter cubes, whisking vigorously. Season to taste.
8. Arrange a nest of greens on attractive serving plates and top with the liver slices. Drizzle with the sauce and serve with croutons.

Note:

Other waterfowl livers may be used with the snow goose livers to complete the required quantity.

Grilled Goose
with Mango Barley Salad

Ingredients

1 cup	uncooked barley	250 ml
1 1/3 lb	boned snow goose breasts	600 g
1	red onion, chopped	1
2	Italian tomatoes, cubed *or*	2
1 cup	cherry tomato halves	250 ml
1	avocado, cubed	1
1/2	mango, cut into small cubes	1/2
	juice of 1/2 lemon	
1 tsp or more	ground cumin	5 ml or more
	salt and freshly ground pepper to taste	

Method

1. Preheat the barbecue to medium-high.
2. Cook the barley in a large quantity of salted water. Drain, rinse and let cool.
3. Meanwhile, cook the goose breasts on a greased barbecue grill for 10 minutes each side.
4. Mix the barley with the onion, tomatoes, avocado and mango. Stir in the lemon juice and the cumin. Season to taste.
5. Place the breasts, whole or sliced, on a nest of the barley salad and serve with homemade mayonnaise.

Rhubarb-Goose Fusion

4 SERVINGS

Ingredients

1 1/3 lb	Canada goose breasts	600 g
1 tbsp	oil	15 ml
2	shallots, chopped	2
2 tbsp	wine vinegar	30 ml
1/4 cup	sugar	60 ml
3/4 cup	cubed fresh rhubarb	180 ml
1 1/3 cups	goose stock (see recipe on page 7)	330 ml
2 tbsp	flour	30 ml
2 tbsp	butter	30 ml
	salt and freshly ground pepper to taste	

Method

1. Using an ovenproof skillet, sear the goose breasts, skin-side first, over medium heat for 5 to 7 minutes per side. Remove and keep warm.

2. Meanwhile, heat the oil in a saucepan and cook the shallots for 2 or 3 minutes.

3. Remove from the heat and deglaze with the vinegar. Add the sugar, return to the heat and caramelize over low heat.

4. Add the rhubarb and stock. Cook over medium heat for 10 to 15 minutes.

5. Meanwhile, combine the flour and butter to make a *beurre manié,* and add to the sauce, whisking vigorously until the sauce thickens.

6. Using a food processor or mixer, purée the sauce until smooth. Season to taste. Return the sauce to the saucepan and simmer until desired thickness is obtained.

7. Serve the goose breasts coated with the rhubarb sauce.

Curried Honey Goose Casserole

Ingredients

1 tbsp	oil	15 ml
1 1/3 lb	snow goose pieces, bone in	600 g
1	onion, sliced	1
2 tbsp	curry paste	30 ml
1 tbsp	chopped garlic	15 ml
3 tbsp	honey	45 ml
1 cup	coconut milk	250 ml
2	carrots, julienned	2
1	yellow or red pepper, julienned	1
1	zucchini, julienned	1
1 cup	snow peas	250 ml
	salt and freshly ground pepper to taste	

Method

1. Preheat the oven to 375°F (190°C).

2. Heat the oil in a skillet and brown the goose and the onion. Transfer to an ovenproof dish.

3. Add the curry paste, garlic, honey and coconut milk. Season to taste. Cover and bake in the oven for 30 minutes.

4. Add the vegetables and continue baking for 10 minutes. Season to taste. Serve with basmati rice.

Roast Goose

Ingredients

Marinade

1	onion, finely chopped	1
2	cloves garlic, crushed	2
1	stalk celery, finely chopped	1
1	carrot, finely shredded	1
1 tbsp	dried savory	15 ml
1 tsp	dried thyme	5 ml
1 tsp	dried oregano	5 ml
	juice of 2 lemons	
1/4 cup	oil	60 ml
	freshly ground pepper to taste	

Goose

1	snow goose, whole	1
1 cup	poultry stock	250 ml
1/2 cup	white wine	125 ml
1 to 2 tbsp	cornstarch	15 to 30 ml

Method

1. Combine all the marinade ingredients in a shallow dish, using half the lemon juice. Season to taste.

2. Rub the goose with the remaining lemon juice. Place in the marinade, cover and marinate in the refrigerator at least 30 minutes, and up to 4 hours, turning the meat frequently.

3. Preheat the oven to 350°F (180°C).

4. Remove the goose from the marinade and place in a roasting pan.

5. In a bowl, combine the stock and the wine. Brush the goose with this mixture and cook in the center of the oven for 60 to 90 minutes. Baste often with the rest of the wine mixture.

6. Remove the goose. Save the cooking juices and skim off excess grease.

7. Bring to a boil and thicken with the cornstarch mixed with a bit of cold water. Serve the roast goose with the thickened pan juices.

Goose with Wild Rice Stuffing

Ingredients

Stuffing

2 cups	cooked wild rice	500 mL
2 cups	cooked white rice	500 ml
1	onion, finely chopped	1
1	clove garlic, crushed	1
1	stalk celery, finely chopped	1
1	carrot, finely chopped	1
2 tbsp	your choice of chopped fresh herbs	30 ml
	juice of 1 lemon	
1/2 cup	brown waterfowl stock (see recipe on page 7)	125 ml
1	Canada goose, whole	1

Sauce

1 cup	brown waterfowl stock	250 ml
2 tbsp	your choice of chopped fresh herbs	30 ml
	salt and freshly ground pepper to taste	

Method

1. Preheat the oven to 400°F (200°C).

2. Mix all stuffing ingredients together in a bowl with half of the stock. Season to taste.

3. Stuff the goose cavity with this mixture and place in a greased ovenproof dish.

4. Brush the goose with the remaining stock and cook in the center of the oven for 45 to 60 minutes. Baste again twice during cooking.

5. Turn the oven off, remove the cooking juices and set aside. Return the goose to the oven.

6. To make the sauce, degrease the cooking juices in a small saucepan, mix with the stock and reduce by half or until desired consistency.

7. Add the fresh herbs and season to taste. Serve the goose with a vegetable julienne and the herb sauce.

Horseradish-Flavored Goose Stew

Ingredients

3 tbsp	oil	45 ml
1	Canada goose, at least	
	4 lb (2 kg), cut into 8 pieces	1
1	onion, chopped	1
3	carrots, cut into sections	3
3	stalks celery, sliced	3
1 cup	white wine	250 ml
3 cups	goose stock	750 ml
	chopped fresh horseradish to taste	
1	bay leaf	1
pinch	dried thyme	pinch
2	cloves	2
6	potato, quartered	6
1/4 cup	chopped fresh parsley	60 ml
	salt and freshly ground pepper to taste	

Method

1. In a large pot, heat the oil over high heat and brown the goose pieces. Remove and set aside.

2. In the same pot, sauté the vegetables over medium heat.

3. Deglaze with the wine and add the goose pieces and the remaining ingredients, except for the potato and parsley. Bring to a boil and simmer, uncovered, for 1 hour. Season to taste.

4. Add the potatoes and continue cooking for 20 to 30 minutes.

5. Season to taste and serve immediately, accompanied with fresh country-style bread.

Note:

For more texture, thicken the sauce with a *beurre manié*.

Orchard Ragoût

Ingredients

2 tbsp	oil	30 ml
1 tbsp	butter	15 ml
	flour for dredging	
1 1/3 lb	boned and cubed Canada goose meat	600 g
1	leek, white part only, chopped	1
2	cloves garlic, chopped	2
1 1/4 cup	dry cider	2/3 cup
1 1/3 cup	waterfowl stock	330 ml
1	bay leaf	1
1 or 2	orchard fruits of your choice, chopped (apples, peaches, pears, apricots, plums, etc.)	1 or 2
1/4 cup	35% cream (optional)	60 ml
	salt and freshly ground pepper to taste	

Method

1. Heat the oil and butter in a saucepan over high heat.
2. Dredge the meat cubes in the flour, shaking off any excess. Sear the meat in the fat.
3. Add the leek and garlic and continue cooking for several minutes.
4. Deglaze with the cider and reduce over low heat.
5. Add the stock, bring to a boil and simmer for about 1 hour or until the meat is tender. Add the bay leaf and season to taste about 20 minutes before the meat is done.
6. When the meat is tender, add the chopped fruit and cream and reheat for 3 or 4 minutes.
7. Remove the bay leaf and serve immediately over a bed of fried leeks.

Goose Stuffed
with Grilled Vegetables

Ingredients

Grilled vegetables

1/4 cup	oil	**60 ml**
1	clove garlic, minced	**1**
1 tbsp	fresh parsley, chopped	**15 ml**
2 tbsp	chopped fresh oregano or other herb (basil, thyme, rosemary, etc.)	**30 ml**
2	zucchini, sliced lengthwise in 1/4-in. (1/2 cm) slices	**2**
2	yellow peppers, cut into strips	**2**
1	portobello mushroom, sliced	**1**
	salt and freshly ground pepper to taste	

2 tbsp	oil	**30 ml**
1 1/3 lb	boned Canada goose breasts	**600 g**
	salt and freshly ground pepper to taste	

Method

1. Preheat the barbecue to medium-high or the oven to 425°F (210°C).

2. In a bowl, combine the oil, garlic, parsley, oregano, and salt and pepper. Add the vegetables and stir well to coat.

3. Place the vegetables on a baking sheet and cook on the grill or in the oven for 10 to 15 minutes, until tender. Turn several times during cooking to brown evenly. Set aside.

4. Slice open the goose breasts without completely separating them. Place the grilled vegetables inside the breast cavity, fold closed and secure with toothpicks. Season generously.

5. Preheat the oven to 375°F (180°C). Heat the oil in a skillet and sear the breasts on both sides. Transfer to an ovenproof dish and continue cooking in the oven or on the barbecue grill for 10 to 15 minutes, according to size.

6. Slice the breasts and arrange in a fan shape on individual plates, accompanied with a green salad.

Goose Wellington

Ingredients

1 tbsp	oil	15 ml
1 tbsp	butter	15 ml
2	snow goose breasts	2
1/2 lb	snow goose liver	225 g
2 tbsp	cognac or brandy	30 ml
1/2 lb	commercial puff pastry, rolled to 1/2-in. (1.2-cm) thickness	225 g
1	egg, beaten	1
	salt and freshly ground pepper to taste	

Method

1. Preheat the oven to 425°F (210°C).

2. Heat the oil and butter in a skillet and sear the breasts and goose livers.

3. Add the cognac and flambé carefully with a match. Shake the skillet until the flames are extinguished.

4. Remove the meat and allow to cool.

5. Cut the puff pastry into two sections. Place the breasts in the center of one of the pastry sections and top with the cooked liver. Season to taste.

6. Brush the pastry with the beaten egg. Cover with the other pastry section and trim the edges.

7. Brush the top with the beaten egg and cook in the center of the oven for about 20 minutes, or until the pastry is a deep golden color.

8. Remove from the oven and let stand for 10 minutes before serving with your favorite sauce.

Orange Goose Supreme

Ingredients

1 1/3 lb	snow goose breasts	600 g
1 tbsp	oil	15 ml
1	shallot, minced	
1/3 cup	orange liqueur (Grand Marnier, Triple Sec, Cointreau, etc.)	80 ml
	juice and zest of 1 orange	
1 cup	35% whipping cream or 15% cooking cream	250 ml
2 tbsp	chopped fresh basil	30 ml
	salt and freshly ground pepper to taste	

Method

1. Preheat the oven to 375°F (190°C).

2. Heat the oil in a skillet and quickly sear the goose breasts. Season with salt and pepper. Transfer to an ovenproof dish and place in the oven for about 20 minutes.

3. Meanwhile, sauté the shallot in the same skillet.

4. Deglaze with the liqueur, add the orange juice and reduce by a third.

5. Heat the cream with a bit of the hot orange mixture and pour into the skillet. Simmer for several minutes until desired thickness.

6. At the last minute, add the orange zest and the basil, and season to taste .

7. Serve the goose coated with the orange sauce, accompanied with a starchy food and seasonal vegetables.

Traditional Goose Stew

Ingredients

1 1/3 lb	Canada goose meat, cubed	600 g
2 L	goose stock or water	8 cups
2	carrots, cubed	2
1	onion, chopped	1
2	stalks celery, cubed	2
2	cloves garlic, peeled	2
1/2 tsp	dried thyme	2 ml
5 to 10	whole peppercorns	5 to 10
1	bay leaf	1
1/4 cup	butter	60 ml
1/2 cup	pearl onions, fresh or frozen	125 ml
1/2 cup	quartered mushrooms	125 ml
1/4 cup	flour	60 ml
1/2 cup	35% whipping cream	125 ml
	juice of 1 lemon	
	salt and freshly ground pepper to taste	

Method

1. Place the goose meat cubes in a saucepan and cover with water.

2. Bring to a boil and simmer for 10 minutes. Drain and cool under cold running water.

3. Return the cubes to the saucepan, add the stock or water, the vegetables and herbs, and return to a boil. Season to taste and simmer over low heat for 20 to 30 minutes, or until the meat is tender.

4. Remove the meat from the cooking stock, discard the vegetables and set aside 5 cups (1 1/4 liters) of the stock. Discard the remaining stock

5. In the same saucepan, heat the butter over medium-high heat and sauté the pearl onions and mushrooms. Remove and set aside. Add the flour to the saucepan and continue cooking until the flour begins to brown.

6. Gradually add the reserved stock, stirring constantly. Bring to a boil and simmer for 30 minutes. Add the onions, mushrooms and goose meat cubes and continue cooking for 10 minutes.

7. Add the cream and lemon juice, and season to taste.

   Serve the stew immediately, accompanied with your favorite potato dish.

Goose Croquettes

Ingredients

1 tbsp	butter	15 ml
1/2	onion, chopped	1/2
1/2 cup	chopped mushrooms	125 ml
1 1/3 lb	cooked, chopped snow goose meat	600 g
2 tbsp	commercial cream of chicken	30 ml
2 tbsp	parsley	30 ml
	salt and freshly ground pepper to taste	
1/4 cup	flour	60 ml
1	beaten egg	1
1/4 cup	breadcrumbs	60 ml
	oil	

Method

1. Heat the butter in a skillet over high heat and brown the onion and mushrooms until all liquid has evaporated.

2. Transfer to a bowl and add the cooked goose, cream of chicken and the parsley. Season to taste, mix well and cover and refrigerate for at least 30 minutes.

3. Shape into eight croquettes.

4. Dust the croquettes with the flour, shaking off any excess, and dip them in the beaten egg mixture before coating with the breadcrumbs.

5. Fry the croquettes in a deep fryer, drain well and serve immediately, accompanied with your favorite garnish.

Pesto Ragoût

Ingredients

Pesto

2	cloves garlic	2
1/4 cup	toasted pine nuts or almonds	60 ml
1 cup	your choice of fresh herbs (basil, lemon balm, tarragon, parsley, oregano)	250 ml
1/4 cup	grated Parmesan	60 ml
1/2 cup	olive oil	125 ml
	salt and freshly ground pepper to taste	

Ragoût

1 tbsp	oil	15 ml
1 1/3 lb	cubed snow goose meat	600 g
2	shallots, chopped	2
1/4 cup	white wine	60 ml
1 cup	goose stock	250 ml
3 tbsp	pesto	45 ml
1/2 cup	35% whipping cream	125 ml
	salt and freshly ground pepper to taste	

Method

1. Use a food processor to prepare the pesto: chop the garlic with the nuts.

2. Add the herbs, Parmesan cheese, salt and pepper. Continue processing this mixture until the herbs are finely chopped.

3. With the food processor running, add the olive oil in a thin stream until desired consistency is obtained. Season to taste and store the pesto in the refrigerator.

4. Preheat the oven to 350°F (180°C).

5. Heat the oil in an ovenproof dish over high heat and sear the goose meat cubes.

6. Add the shallots and continue cooking for 2 minutes.

7. Deglaze with the white wine and reduce by half.

8. Add the stock, season to taste, cover and bake in the oven for 30 to 45 minutes, or until the meat cubes are tender.

9. Add the pesto and the cream, stirring constantly. Serve immediately.

Leg of Goose
in an Almond Crust

Ingredients

1/4 cup	Dijon mustard	**60 ml**
2 tbsp	honey	**30 ml**
4	Canada goose legs, skin removed	**4**
1/2 cup	sliced almonds	**125 ml**
	salt and freshly ground pepper to taste	

Method

1. Preheat the oven to 350°F (180°C).
2. Combine the mustard and honey in a bowl. Season to taste.
3. Coat the goose legs with the mustard mixture and roll in the almonds.
4. Transfer to a baking sheet and bake in the oven for 45 to 60 minutes, or until the meat separates easily from the bone.
5. Serve immediately, accompanied with your favorite garnish.

Goose Enchiladas

Ingredients

2 tbsp	oil	30 ml
1	pepper of your choice, cut into strips	1
1	onion, sliced	1
1 or 2	cloves garlic, minced	1 or 2
1 tsp	chili powder	5 ml
1/2 tsp	ground cumin	2 ml
1/2 tsp	ground coriander	2 ml
1 lb	cooked Canada goose, cut into strips	500 g
	salt and freshly ground pepper to taste	
4	large tortillas	4
1/2 cup	salsa	125 ml
1 cup	tomato sauce	250 ml
1 cup	grated cheese (Monterey Jack, Mozzarella, etc.)	250 ml

Method

1. Preheat the oven to 400°F (200°C).

2. In a skillet, heat the oil over medium-high heat and sauté the vegetables for 4 to 5 minutes.

3. Add the spices, coating the vegetables well. Add the goose and season to taste.

4. Divide the mixture among the four tortillas, roll up and place in an ovenproof dish.

5. Combine the salsa with the tomato sauce and pour over the enchiladas.

6. Top with cheese and bake for 10 to 15 minutes, or until the cheese begins to turn golden.

7. Serve immediately, accompanied with sour cream and corn chips.

Goose Breast with Prosciutto

Ingredients

1 tbsp	oil	**15 ml**
1 tbsp	butter	**15 ml**
1 1/3 lb	boned Canada goose breasts	**600 g**
4 to 8	slices prosciutto or Bayonne ham	**4 to 8**
	freshly ground pepper to taste	

Method

1. Preheat the oven to 350°F (180°C).

2. Heat the oil and butter in a skillet over high heat.

3. Sear the breasts on both sides, turning only once.

4. Remove the breasts, season with fresh ground pepper and roll each in Prosciutto.

5. Add fresh ground pepper and roll with the prosciutto. Place in an ovenproof dish and cook for 10 to 15 minutes, depending on the size of the breasts.

6. Slice the goose breasts and serve with a seasonal vegetable salad.

Shore Birds

In the days of market hunting, some types of shore birds, most notably curlews, along with golden and upland plovers, were in great demand among epicures in major American cities. Those days are long gone, and some shore birds remain off limits to hunters because their numbers have been so dramatically reduced. Still, in many areas, hunting gallinules, rails and snipe remains legal.

There are two types of gallinule (Florida and purple gallinules), three members of the rail family (sora, clapper and Virginia rails), and three varieties of snipe (greater yellow-legs, lesser yellowlegs and Wilson's snipe). All of these species have nicknames that often vary from one region to another, occasionally resulting in confusion. For example, the sora rail is also called the Carolina rail, Carolina crake, chicken-billed rail, meadow chick, mud hen soree, rail-bird and ortolan. Regardless of the name, they offer a challenging quarry for the hunter and delectable fare for the game gourmet.

While the generic description "shore bird" is accurate in that these birds are commonly found along shorelines, they also frequent wetlands further inland. This means you do not have to live near the sea in order to hunt and eat these delicacies. Most are quite small, and their erratic flight makes them a challenging target, but a limit of shore birds will provide ample "raw material" for a feast. Snipe are small birds that weigh about four ounces and are quite similar in taste to woodcock. The traditional French method of cooking them involves dry-plucking the bird and leaving it undrawn. Individual servings will require at least two snipe. Sora rails also weigh only four or five ounces, but clapper rails can weigh from 10 to 14 ounces, and a single bird makes a decent-sized meal. The coot is also a member of the *rallidae* family. While not normally described as a shorebird, the mud hen, as it is also known, is an underused game bird that tastes delicious if care is taken to remove the skin and all fat.

Shore birds, when properly prepared, are a true delight on the table. They offer a grand opportunity to return to the kind of dining enjoyed in simpler days and simpler ways. The recipes in this book will enable you to turn back the clock to enjoy a genteel aspect of our culinary past.

Rail Cacciatore

Ingredients

2 tbsp	oil	30 ml
1 tbsp	butter	15 ml
	flour seasoned with salt and pepper	
1	rail, cut into eight pieces	1
2	shallots, chopped	2
2 cups	sliced mushrooms	500 ml
1/4 cup	brandy or cognac	60 ml
1/2 cup	dry white wine	125 ml
2 cups	brown waterfowl stock (see recipe on page 7)	500 ml
3 tbsp	tomato paste	45 ml
	salt and freshly ground pepper to taste	
1 to 2 tbsp	fresh parsley, chopped	15 to 30 ml
2 tsp	chopped fresh tarragon	10 ml
1 tbsp	chopped fresh basil	15 ml

Method

1. Preheat the oven to 350°F (180°C).

2. Heat the oil and butter in a skillet over high heat.

3. Dust the rail pieces with the flour and sear them in the oil and butter. Transfer to a casserole dish.

4. In the same skillet, brown the shallots and mushrooms.

5. Deglaze with the brandy and wine, and reduce by a third.

6. Add the stock and stir in the tomato paste. Season generously to taste. Bring to a boil and simmer for 5 minutes.

7. Pour the sauce into the casserole dish, cover and bake in the center of the oven for 30 to 45 minutes.

8. Add the fresh herbs just before serving.

Common Snipe with Kumquats And Ginger

Ingredients

1	common snipe, quartered	1
1 tbsp	chopped fresh ginger	15 ml
1 cup	sliced and seeded kumquats	250 ml
1/3 cup	honey	80 ml
2/3 cup	orange juice	160 ml
	salt and freshly ground pepper to taste	

Method

1. Preheat the oven to 400°F (200°C).

2. Place the snipe pieces in an ovenproof dish.

3. Combine the ginger with the kumquats, honey and orange juice. Season to taste.

4. Pour this mixture over the snipe and cook in the center of the oven for 20 to 30 minutes.

5. Serve immediately, accompanied with a green salad.

Note:

You can also prepare this recipe in advance by combining all ingredients and cooking the next day. This also allows the snipe to marinate in the mixture, making it tastier and more tender.

Common Snipe in Cider

Ingredients

2 tbsp	oil	30 ml
4	common snipe breasts	4
1 or 2	shallots, sliced	1 or 2
2 tbsp	flour	30 ml
1/2 cup	dry cider	125 ml
1 cup	brown waterfowl stock (see recipe on page 7)	250 ml
	salt and freshly ground pepper to taste	
1/2	apple, peel on, finely diced	1/2

Method

1. Preheat the oven to 375°F (190°C).

2. Heat the oil in a large skillet and sear the snipe breasts, fat side down first, for 2 or 3 minutes each side, depending on thickness. Place in an ovenproof dish and continue cooking in the oven for 15 minutes.

3. Meanwhile, sauté the shallots in the same skillet. Dust with the flour and mix well to make a roux.

4. Deglaze with the cider and add the stock, stirring constantly. Season to taste and simmer until desired consistency is obtained.

5. Serve the snipe breasts coated with the sauce and accompanied with the diced apple.

Coot Breast Stuffed with Crab

4 SERVINGS

Ingredients

1 cup	shredded crab	250 ml
1 tbsp	tomato paste	15 ml
1	shallot, minced	1
1	clove garlic, crushed	1
2 tbsp	breadcrumbs	30 ml
pinch	cayenne	pinch
1 tbsp	chopped fresh basil, or pesto	15 ml
1 tbsp	chopped fresh oregano	15 ml
1	egg	1
1 cup	35% cream	250 ml
4	coot breasts, boned	4
1 cup	brown waterfowl stock	250 ml
	salt and freshly ground pepper, to taste	

Method

1. Preheat the grill or the oven to 350°F (180°C).

2. Using a food processor, purée the crab with half the tomato paste, the shallot, garlic, pepper, basil and oregano to obtain a smooth paste.

3. Add the egg and 1/4 cup (60 ml) cream. Season to taste generously and set aside.

4. Cut the breasts open to form a pocket and flatten with a butcher's mallet or a skillet.

5. Divide the stuffing among the breasts, fold over and attach using toothpicks. Place in a greased ovenproof dish. Add the stock, cover and cook in the center of the oven for 20 to 25 minutes.

6. Pour off the cooking juices, transfer to a saucepan and reduce by half.

7. Add the remaining tomato paste and cream. Simmer until smooth and creamy. Season to taste.

8. Slice the coot breasts, arrange on dinner plates and top with the sauce. Serve with green vegetables of your choice.

Snipe Vol-au-Vent

Ingredients

1 tbsp	oil	15 ml
1 tbsp	butter	15 ml
1 lb	cubed common snipe	500 g
1	onion, chopped	1
1	carrot, cubed	1
1	stalk celery, cubed	1
1/2 cup	green beans, cut in sections	125 ml
1 cup	waterfowl stock	250 ml
2 tbsp	flour	30 ml
2 tbsp	butter	30 ml
1/4 cup	35% cream	60 ml
4	large store-bought vol-au-vent shells*	4
	or	
8	small store-bought vol-au-vent shells	8
	salt and freshly ground pepper to taste	

Method

1. Preheat the oven to 400°F (200°C).
2. Heat the oil and butter in a saucepan over high heat and brown the snipe meat cubes. Remove and set aside.
3. In the same saucepan, cook the vegetables over medium heat.
4. Add the snipe, moisten with the stock and season to taste. Cover and simmer for 25 to 30 minutes over low heat.
5. Combine the butter with the flour to make a *beurre manié*. Add the *beurre manié* to the stock using a wooden spoon, stirring constantly.
6. Stir in the cream and season to taste.
7. Meanwhile, cook the vol-au-vent in the oven as per package instructions. Remove and serve the vol-au-vent filled with the sauce.

★ Lidded puff pastry shells.

Coot à la Florentine

Ingredients

4	coot legs	4
2 tbsp	oil	30 ml
1 tbsp	butter	15 ml
1/4 cup	chopped shallots	60 ml
1/2 lb	fresh spinach, chopped	225 g
1/2 cup	white wine	125 ml
1 cup	35% cream	250 ml
	salt and freshly ground pepper to taste	

Method

1. Preheat the oven to 400°F (200°C).

2. Place the legs on a baking sheet, brush with the oil and season to taste. Cook in the center of the oven for 35 to 40 minutes, or until the meat separates easily from the bone.

3. Heat the butter in a saucepan and cook the shallots over medium heat.

4. Add the spinach and pour in the white wine. Cook until tender, for 2 or 3 minutes.

5. Stir in the cream and reduce by half. Season to taste.

6. Serve the legs coated with the sauce, and accompanied with your favorite vegetables.

Rail with Figs

Ingredients

1 tbsp	oil	15 ml
2 tbsp	butter	30 ml
1	rail, cut into morsels	1
2	shallots, chopped	2
2 tbsp	flour	30 ml
1/4 cup	red wine	60 ml
1 1/2 cups	waterfowl stock	375 ml
1/4 cup	sliced or chopped dried figs	60 ml
	salt and freshly ground pepper to taste	

Method

1. Preheat the oven to 400°F (200°C).

2. Heat the oil and butter in a skillet.

3. Sear the rail pieces on all sides. Place in an ovenproof dish and bake for 20 to 35 minutes, or until the meat separates easily from the bone.

4. Meanwhile, cook the shallots in the same skillet. Dust with flour to obtain a roux.

5. Deglaze with the red wine, add with the stock and bring to a boil.

6. Add the figs and simmer over low heat to desired consistency or until the figs are tender. Season to taste.

7. Serve the legs coated with the sauce.

Stuffed Breast of Moor Hen with a Honey Glaze

4 SERVINGS

Ingredients

Stuffing

1/2 lb	chopped poultry meat	225 g
1	egg	1
1/2 cup	chopped onion	125 ml
2	cloves garlic, minced	2
2 tbsp	breadcrumbs	30 ml
1/2 tsp	dried savory	2 ml
1/2 tsp	dried thyme	2 ml
2 tsp	honey	10 ml
1 tbsp	oil	15 ml
1 1/3 lb	moor hen breasts	600 g

Sauce

1 1/2 tbsp	butter	22 ml
1 tbsp	flour	15 ml
1 1/2 cups	brown waterfowl stock (see recipe on page 7)	375 ml
1 to 2 tbsp	honey	15 to 30 ml
	salt and freshly ground pepper to taste	

Method

1. Preheat the oven to 350°F (180°C).
2. Combine all stuffing ingredients and season to taste.
3. Cut the breasts open to form a pocket, without separating completely.
4. Divide the stuffing among the breasts, fold over and secure using toothpicks.
5. Heat the oil in a skillet and sear the breasts. Transfer to an ovenproof dish and bake in the oven for about 25 minutes.
6. Meanwhile, using the same skillet, heat the butter and dust with the flour to obtain a roux. Cook over medium heat until the flour begins to brown.
7. Add the stock, whisking vigorously with a wire whisk. Bring to a boil and reduce by about a third or until desired consistency is obtained.
8. Stir in the honey and season to taste.
9. Ladle a serving of sauce on each dinner plate and place the moor hen breasts on top, whole or cut in two.

Index